Workbook: Atomic Habits

An Implementation Guide to James Clear's Book: Atomic Habits: An Easy and Proven Way to Build Good Habits & Break Bad Ones

Inspirational Creator

ISBN 978-1-922940-186 (E-book)
ISBN 978-1-922940-193 (Paperback)
ISBN 978-1-922940-209 (Hardcover)

Cover Design by Sezt
Published by Inspirational Creator
Liam Daniels
First Edition (2023)

YOUR FREE GIFT

As a **thank you** for your purchase, and to further supplement your learning, we're offering the book *'The Habits of Highly Joyful People'* completely free.

To get your copy visit *inspirationalcreator.com* or alternatively scan the QR Code below.

Get ready to discover:

- the big difference this little book can make
- the keys to happiness and myths to debunk
- how to foster warm, authentic relationships with one question
- and so much more!

If you want to dig deeper into the science of joy and happiness, make sure to grab the free book.

In addition to the GIFT, you'll also have access to exclusive giveaways, discounts, and other valuable information.

Table of Contents

Why You Need This Workbook

Firstly, it must be reiterated that this is not the original book *Atomic Habits* by James Clear. It is a workbook, designed to be an accompanying guide to Clear's work. It summarizes the key ideas and messages of *Atomic Habits* and provides exercises for you to put Clear's theories into action.

You might be thinking, "So why do I need this workbook? I can just read the original." True—and in fact, please do—it's a brilliant read. This workbook will then serve as a refresher and help you implement all the ideas and suggestions that Clear makes. But it may be that you don't have the time, motivation, or energy to read the whole book right now. Don't worry, you wouldn't be the first. In fact, did you know that 60 percent of purchased e-books are never even opened? And those that *are* opened are often only read 20-40 percent of the way through.

This workbook will make sure that you gain full knowledge of Clear's concepts, whether you get around to reading his book or not. Its interactive nature allows you to take regular breaks to write things down and practice implementing what you've just read. And guess what? You're 42 percent more likely to achieve your goals if you write them down.

This is why you need this workbook. It's a great resource to have if you want the main takeaways from Clear's book and a quick and easy reference guide for how to implement them. Whether it's for personal health, relationships, money, or any other area of life, this book will help you make real changes that last. Please note that all page number references throughout this workbook are in reference to Clear's *Atomic Habits*.

As a final note, please feel free to use the examples given throughout this workbook (in the chapter summaries and the exercise sections) as inspiration. Several are taken from Clear's book, but many are from the author's own mind. For this same reason it is important to remember that you can personalize the exercises as much as you need to. You will get more out of it if you implement what is most relevant and meaningful to you.

Introduction: James Clear's Story

Clear begins his story by detailing a serious injury he had in his second year of high school. During a baseball game, his face was crushed by a flying baseball bat, majorly concussing him and eventually leading to an induced coma. Luckily, one week and a surgical operation later, Clear was able to leave the hospital.

He describes his long, slow recovery, particularly his painful return to high school baseball. Despite having played all his life, he was now unable to make the varsity team and suffered the humiliation of being downgraded. He didn't let this get him down, however, and as high school ended and university began, Clear decided to face this new chapter with a fresh determination.

It was at university that Clear first discovered "the surprising power of small habits" (p. 11). This was the breakthrough. During his freshman year, Clear learned that going to bed early and keeping his dorm room tidy improved his confidence and sense of control. This, in turn, inspired him to study regularly and start lifting weights. Before long, he was a straight-A student and captain of the baseball team. It all culminated in his final year, when he was selected for the "ESPN Academic All-America Team" and "awarded the university's highest academic honor, the President's Medal" (p. 12).

Clear continued to reap the benefits of his disciplined habits long after his education. The journey to writing *Atomic Habits*, for example, began with Clear publishing two articles a week on his website. That was in 2012. Within three years, this "simple writing habit" (p. 13) had attracted over two hundred thousand email subscribers. Today, he has over two million subscribers, with millions more visiting his website every month.

Following popular demand to appear and speak at top companies and sports associations, Clear founded the Habits Academy in 2017. It quickly became the top training platform for individuals, start-ups, and international organizations wanting to build better habits and generally improve their lives and work. The number of graduates from the Habits Academy is now in the tens of thousands. As Clear notes himself in the introduction to his book, this result is "so far beyond my expectations when I began that I'm not even sure what to think of it" (p. 14).

In telling his story, Clear wants to demonstrate how a remarkable ripple effect can be initiated by small, regular improvements to your life. Far from being an abstract philosophy, his strategies and principles have come from his own lived experience. He is living proof that they work.

Atomic Habits draws on knowledge that has been around for a while. It synthesizes well-known research, recent scientific discoveries, and practical advice into an easy-to-follow manual full of actionable ideas. Where its approach is new, however, is in Clear's focus on internal stimuli for our habits—namely emotions, thought processes, and belief systems. Hitherto, behavioral science had focused mainly on external stimuli as influencers of our habits. By combining the two, Clear creates a groundbreaking model of human behavior that will change the way you think about your habits.

In the introduction, Clear presents his two key concepts for understanding habit formation. These are the "four-step model of habits—cue, craving, response, and reward" and "the four laws of behavior change" (p. 15). Together, they make up the structural and ideological foundation of Clear's training. This workbook will follow the same structure as *Atomic Habits* and will break down and explain each concept as it arises.

Fundamentals: Why Tiny Changes Make a Big Difference

Chapter 1: The Surprising Power of Atomic Habits

Chapter Summary

In this chapter, Clear introduces the concept of one percent improvement. Too often, we think that change comes from a single defining moment. We put a huge amount of pressure on ourselves to improve quickly, expecting to see results right away. When this inevitably doesn't happen, we lose motivation and give up.

But what if you aimed to get better by just one percent every day? It might not seem like much at first, but over a significant period of time, small improvements can accumulate into remarkable change. For example, if you are a student and you want to improve your grades, you might take the following steps:

1. Turn off all electronic devices 30 minutes before bed to improve your quality of sleep.
2. Put your phone on airplane mode while working to avoid distractions.
3. Take regular study breaks (perhaps even a nap) to avoid fatigue.

You could make similar improvements to your diet and your exercise routine, but remember to introduce them gradually, little by little. Clear has a formula for this. He calculates that if you improve by one percent every day for a year, you will be thirty-seven times better than when you started. This works the other way too. If you get worse by one percent every day for a year, you'll end up at zero.

In other words, it's about looking at the bigger picture. Saving a bit of money each month might not seem worth it in the moment, but ten years down the line you may find yourself in a better position to buy a house or set up a company. Conversely, spending more than you earn each month might not seem like a problem if you're a millionaire, but with enough repetition, you will eventually run out of money. This is a crucial point that Clear wants his readers to understand. Habits can compound for you or against you. Deciding to improve or worsen your daily habits by one percent today will determine who you become in the future.

A key analogy that Clear uses in this chapter is the melting of an ice cube. Imagine you are in a room at 25 °F. In front of you is a table with an ice cube on top. The room slowly starts to heat up, degree by degree, until it reaches 31 °F. The ice cube remains unchanged. The room increases to 32 °F. Suddenly, the ice cube begins to melt. Although the temperature only shifted by one degree, it triggered a big change.

The same is true for building habits. Eventually, there comes a turning point where the small improvements you have been making start to become noticeable in a big way. Before this happens, it is easy to get frustrated and disheartened by the lack of results. Clear calls this the Valley of Disappointment (p. 23). Within this valley is the Plateau of Latent Potential (p. 24). This refers to the period of time in which your efforts are being invisibly stacked on top of each other like the degrees melting the ice cube. You may not be seeing results yet, but your actions are not in vain; it just takes that one extra day of practicing your habit to unlock tremendous results. At this point, Clear warns his readers not to mistake this breakthrough for an overnight success. It is simply your patience paying off.

Another main concept that Clear introduces in this chapter is the importance of systems. He breaks away from the common advice that setting goals is the best way to achieve results and tells his readers to focus on changing their systems instead. So what's the difference between a system and a goal? A goal is *what* you want to achieve, i.e., the final result. A system is *how* you achieve it, i.e., the process you went through to get there.

Here are some examples that Clear gives:

Type of Person	Their Goal	Their System
Basketball coach.	To win the championship.	How they scout and recruit players, conduct team practice sessions, and manage their assistant coaches.
Entrepreneur.	To set up their own million-dollar business.	How they hire employees, run product tests, and conduct marketing campaigns.
Musician.	To put out a new album.	How often they practice, how they deal with artist's block, and whether they listen to advice from producers.

Clear's point is that you could take the goal out of this equation and focus solely on your system, and you would still be just as successful. In fact, you're probably going to be more successful because you wouldn't be worrying about meeting your goal. He lists four main reasons why goals are unhelpful:

1. A goal does not differentiate a winner from a loser. Both want to win, so simply having a goal is not what leads to success. It is the system you use that determines whether or not you'll get there.

2. The success of meeting a goal is momentary and fleeting. It is easy to mess up your room again after tidying it. Changing your system means you won't have those bad habits in the first place; you will become a tidy person.

3. You risk sacrificing your happiness. When you set a goal you implicitly tell yourself you'll only be happy once you've achieved it. This puts unnecessary and unrealistic pressure on yourself.

4. Setting goals can create "a yo-yo effect" (p. 28). Once you achieve your goal you stop practicing that good habit because there is nothing left to motivate you.

Focusing on systems instead of goals means long-term and long-lasting success. If you are finding it difficult to change your habits, it is most likely a problem with your system, not you.

Clear concludes this chapter with a definition of "atomic habits." He describes it as "a regular practice or routine that is not only small and easy to do, but also the source of incredible power" (p. 29).

Key Takeaways

- Success is achieved through a build-up of small day-to-day improvements repeated over time, not a single defining moment.
- Start small. Aim to improve by one percent each day.
- Visible results are delayed until you break through the Plateau of Latent Potential. You must be patient and persistent.
- Focus on changing your systems (for long-term results) rather than achieving your goals (temporary changes). Goals help you set the direction, but systems will help you progress.

Over to You

Use the space below to brainstorm all of your current habits, separating the positive ones from the negative ones. If you're not sure whether a habit is positive or negative, think about whether it's helpful to you or not. Take your time with this exercise. You might want to play some music or make yourself a hot drink. Whatever you need to make the experience more enjoyable.

Positive	**Negative**

Now make a list of all your goals, starting with those most important to you and ending with the least. In the table below, write down examples of habits that would bring you closer to that goal and ones that would keep you further away. See the first two examples.

Goal	**Habits that bring you closer to this goal**	**Habits that keep you further from this goal**
To learn a new language.	Learning new words and phrases for 15-30 minutes a day. Hanging notes around the house. Watching movies and listening to music in that language. Setting your phone to that language.	No regular practice. Only watching your favorite tv shows and series in your spare time. Always opting to see friends instead of a speaking partner. Generally having no exposure to that

	Trying to regularly converse with a native speaker.	language.
To be a happier person.	Smiling more. Being generous. Practicing gratitude for five minutes each day. Taking time off work to be in nature. Spending time with family and friends. Dancing in your kitchen for 20 minutes every day. Exercising regularly and adopting good sleeping patterns. Decluttering your room.	Frowning and glaring at people. Over-working. Never having enough time to see family or friends. Over-eating. No regular exercise. Letting your room get messy and dirty. Feeling like the world is out to get you.

Now compare the tables from each exercise. Look at your own habits from the first table and see if any of them match the habits listed in the second table. Are you already practicing a habit that will help you achieve your goal? Or hinder you? Which ones do you need to pick up or drop? This is a really useful preliminary exercise because, as you will learn in Chapter 4, the first step towards changing your habits is becoming aware of them.

Write down the habits you decided you needed to pick up or drop and break them down into smaller components. For example, if you want to be more productive with your studying, the components would be: the environment you're working in, when you choose to study and for how long, who you study with, how you will avoid distractions, etc.

For each of these components, identify an action plan to implement small one percent changes that will help build your habit or break it. Afterward, list all of the challenges you went through to either try to build or break that habit.

<table>
<tr><th>Habit</th><th>Components</th><th>Small changes</th></tr>
<tr><td rowspan="6"></td><td rowspan="2"></td><td></td></tr>
<tr><td></td></tr>
<tr><td rowspan="2"></td><td></td></tr>
<tr><td></td></tr>
<tr><td rowspan="2"></td><td></td></tr>
<tr><td></td></tr>
<tr><td colspan="3">Challenges:</td></tr>
</table>

Habit	**Components**	**Small changes**
Challenges:		

Habit	**Components**	**Small changes**
Challenges:		

Chapter 2: How Your Habits Shape Your Identity (and Vice Versa)

Chapter Summary

Clear begins this chapter by addressing that burning question we all ask ourselves: why are bad habits so easy to fall into, and good ones so hard to stick to? It seems that once a habit has established itself, it is near-impossible to kick, especially if it's unhealthy. He says this is due to two reasons. Firstly, when we attempt to change a habit, we focus on the wrong thing. Secondly, we go about it the wrong way.

Clear spends the rest of the chapter getting to the root of the first problem: changing the wrong thing. He explains this using his concept of the "three layers of behavior change" (p. 32). It is helpful to think of change as occurring at three levels: outcomes, processes, and identity. The outermost layer is outcomes. This is where most people start when they create a new habit. Changing your outcomes is like setting a goal. It refers to the results you want to achieve, such as learning to play an instrument or trying to quit drinking. This is generally the least efficient route, as it relies a lot on willpower.

The next layer is processes. This targets change on a deeper level because it involves changing your systems, and as we have seen in the previous chapter, changing your systems is more effective than setting goals. It involves taking action, such as setting aside one hour each day to practice your instrument or signing up for a weekly class at the gym.

The third layer is identity. This is where change can be implemented on the deepest and most life-changing level. Now you are concerned not only with changing your behavior, but also your belief systems and sense of self.

So, if you're trying to build or break a habit and it's not going well, it's likely because you're only targeting your outcomes or processes. Not that there's anything wrong with this. It's natural to begin by focusing on *what* you want to achieve. But what if you took it a step further and went straight to thinking about *who* you want to become?

Clear gives the example of two people who are trying to quit smoking. When offered a cigarette, Person A responds with "No thanks. I'm trying to quit," whereas Person B says "No thanks. I'm not a smoker" (p. 33). The difference between the two is that the former is trying to be someone they don't believe they are. Person B, on the other hand, is identifying as the person they want to be. If you can shift your identity to align with your new habits, you will naturally start to feel proud of them, and they'll become easy to stick with.

As long as your beliefs remain unchanged, it is going to be very difficult to implement real change in your habits. The more you believe in your new identity, the more likely you are to become it. Unfortunately, the power of this transaction can work against you too. We often get roped into versions of ourselves that are so convincing that we believe we are incapable of change. How many times have you heard, "I'm not a morning person" or "I'm terrible with directions" (p. 36)? For this reason, it is very important not to get too attached to any of these particular versions of yourself. They will only get in the way. As Clear says, "progress requires unlearning" (p. 36).

So how do we change our identity? Clear breaks it down. Think of performing a habit as casting a vote to become the type of person associated with that behavior. For example, every time you make the bed, you are voting to be a tidy, organized person. These votes accumulate into a body of evidence, and the more evidence you have to show that you are that type of person, the more likely you are to believe it. You wouldn't consider yourself a musician if you only played the guitar once. But you *would* gradually become a writer if you wrote a page every day. Habits are the building blocks of our identity because of the sheer frequency with which they are repeated throughout our lives.

Once you've understood this, changing your identity becomes "a simple two-step process" (p. 39):

1. Decide on what kind of person you want to be.

2. Build up the evidence needed to prove it to yourself.

Clear concedes that this isn't always as easy as it sounds. Many people don't know who they want to be. If this is you, he says to start with what you want instead. A six-figure salary? Stronger biceps? To feel less stressed? Now think about the kind of person who could achieve those results. Someone who is driven. Consistent. Organized. Put yourself in their shoes and ask yourself, "Would a driven person get their work done or watch TV?" Accordingly, start to make small changes in your behavior to reinforce this new identity. It's like the saying "fake it until you make it," only once you've gathered enough proof, you're no longer faking it because you will have become it. This is the true power of habits.

Key Takeaways

- You can instigate change on three levels: outcomes (what), processes (how), and identity (who).

- Focus on who you want to be and not what you want to achieve (identity-based thinking is key).

- Every time you repeat a habit, you are casting a vote to be the kind of person (identity) associated with that behavior.
- Do not hold yourself back by adhering to one version of yourself. You have the power to change your identity.
- Becoming your desired identity is the biggest motivation for sticking with your habits.

Over to You

Using Clear's concept of the three layers of behavior change, list five of the most important outcomes that you want to achieve. Think about what they would look like on each level. See the first example.

Outcomes	**Processes**	**Identity**
I want to lose weight.	I am going to stop snacking in between meals and go to the gym at least two times a week.	I'm the kind of person who respects their body and values health.

Think about that last column in particular—identity. You have, in effect, just listed five types of people that you want to become. It doesn't matter if these identities overlap or are closely related to each other; this is normal! Now take it a step further and make a list of habits you think each person has. Think of these as the votes they cast to stay as that identity. Make a similar list of habits you think they avoid. Remember, tiny habits count. See the example.

Identity	**Habits they have (votes for)**	**Habits they avoid (votes against)**
The type of person who respects and values their body and health.	They avoid alcohol. If they do drink, it's only occasionally and in small quantities.	Eating junk food. Smoking.

	They have a running buddy whom they meet three times a week. They make a health-boosting smoothie each morning before breakfast. They avoid sugar and salt as much as possible.	Not having enough veggies or water. Spending more than two hours in front of a screen (unless it's for work). Looking in the mirror and thinking they're unattractive.

Becoming the type of person you aspire to requires reflecting on your principles, values, and interests. You can get as creative as you like with these identities. As you write, think about who you are and which votes you could start casting for the person you want to be.

If you are enjoying this book so far, it would mean a lot to me if you could take a minute to review or rate it on the respective platform you acquired it from. Did you know that just 0.5 - 1% of readers do actually end up leaving a review? :)

Chapter 3: How to Build Better Habits in Four Simple Steps

Chapter Summary

Habits arise through a process of trial and error. They are the result of your brain constantly looking for solutions to the daily problems it encounters. Once it finds a solution that works, it logs it and knows how to deal with the situation next time. After this response has been repeated a certain number of times, it becomes automatic, and a habit is formed.

This is why the brain builds habits. They are extremely useful "mental shortcuts" (p. 44) that allow the brain to free up space in its conscious mind so that it can focus on whatever new task is at hand. Clear notes that this process of automation leads some people to associate habits with a dull, predictable life, but they actually do exactly the opposite. Habits take care of the basics for us and enable the mind to follow more creative, challenging pursuits.

To explain how a habit works, Clear breaks it down into four steps: cue, craving, response, and reward (p. 45). The order is always the same:

1. Cue: Your brain sees/hears/experiences something that triggers a certain behavior.
2. Craving: You are filled with a desire to change your current state. This becomes the motivational force to act.
3. Response: You perform the action you know will achieve that change (the habit).

4. Reward: You reach your end goal.

This is what Clear calls a feedback loop or, more specifically, a "habit loop" (p. 48). The first three stages are ultimately concerned with obtaining the reward. This fourth stage gives us a feeling of pleasure and satisfaction, which ensures that the behavior will be repeated. And so the cycle continues.

Clear further divides this process into two phases: "the problem phase and the solution phase" (p. 48):

Problem Phase (When you notice something and feel a desire to change)
1. Cue
2. Craving
Solution Phase (When you take action to solve the problem)
3. Response
4. Reward

When put into a real-life context, the habit loop looks something like this:

Problem Phase
Cue: You walk into a cold room.
Craving: You want to feel warm.
Solution Phase
Response: You put on a sweater.
Reward: You satisfy your craving to feel warm. Putting on a sweater becomes associated with being in a cold room.

After establishing this concept of the four-step cycle, Clear translates it into a set of rules that can be applied to building good habits and breaking bad ones. He calls them the Four Laws of Behavior Change (p. 51).

To build a good habit:

1. The First Law: Make it Obvious (taken from the cue).
2. The Second Law: Make it Attractive (taken from the craving).
3. The Third Law: Make it Easy (taken from the response).
4. The Fourth Law: Make it Satisfying (taken from the reward).

To break a bad habit, you simply invert these four laws:

1. Make it Invisible.
2. Make it Unattractive.
3. Make it Difficult.
4. Make it Unsatisfying.

Clear is confident that you can use this framework to change your behavior in virtually any field.

Key Takeaways

- A habit is a behavior that is repeated regularly enough to become automatic.
- Habits allow your brain to automate as much behavior as possible, ultimately giving your conscious mind the freedom to develop itself.

- To perform a habit, your brain goes through a four-step cycle called a habit loop. This involves a cue, craving, response, and reward.
- Without the cue, craving, and response, a habit will not form. Without the reward, it will not be repeated.
- The four steps translate to the Four Laws of Behavior Change: make it obvious, make it attractive, make it easy, and make it satisfying.

Over to You

Pick three of your positive habits and three of your negative ones. They should be actions that you do automatically or unconsciously. Using the table below, try and complete a habit cycle for each one. Understanding which cues trigger you and what desires motivate you is the key to changing your habits. An example of a positive and negative habit has been given.

Example of a positive habit:

Problem Phase
Cue: I walk into the living room and spot my yoga mat.
Craving: I want to feel stretched and strong.
Solution Phase
Response: I do a 30-minute yoga class.
Reward: I feel wonderful afterward and have satisfied my craving to feel stretched and strong. Doing a 30-minute yoga class becomes associated with entering the living room and spotting my yoga mat.

Positive Habit #1:

Problem Phase
Cue:
Craving:
Solution Phase
Response:
Reward:

Positive Habit #2:

Problem Phase
Cue:
Craving:
Solution Phase
Response:
Reward:

Positive Habit #3:

Problem Phase
Cue:
Craving:

Solution Phase
Response:
Reward:

Example of a negative habit:

Problem Phase
Cue: I wake up.
Craving: I want to stimulate my brain.
Solution Phase
Response: I reach for my phone and check social media.
Reward: I satisfy my craving for brain stimulation and get a dopamine release. Reaching for my phone becomes associated with waking up.

Negative Habit #1:

Problem Phase
Cue:
Craving:
Solution Phase
Response:
Reward:

Negative Habit #2:

Problem Phase
Cue:
Craving:
Solution Phase
Response:
Reward:

Negative Habit #3:

Problem Phase
Cue:
Craving:
Solution Phase
Response:
Reward:

Keep practicing this exercise until you feel you can easily break down any habit into its four steps. Mastering this will help you tremendously in increasing your awareness of habit formation. We will hear more about that in the next chapter.

First Law: Make It Obvious

Chapter 4: The Man Who Didn't Look Right

Chapter Summary

As discussed in the previous chapter, habits become automatic. This means that the brain can notice a cue and set the gears in motion without you ever being aware of it. Although designed to be helpful, this process has its pitfalls. For instance, you might not realize that you have a habit of interrupting people mid-sentence. The more you do it, the less aware you'll be of it, and the more people you'll unwittingly offend.

This is why the first step toward behavior change is awareness. Becoming aware of our habits is Clear's main focus in this chapter. He introduces a helpful technique called Pointing-and-Calling (p. 57), which refers to a process of physically pointing at things and naming them out loud. Studies have found this to be an extremely effective method for reducing margins of error. Clear uses the example of Japanese train operators who point and call their commands, e.g., to indicate a green signal, the speed of the train, or the departure time. You've probably used the technique yourself without realizing it. Have you ever said your mental checklist out loud before leaving the house? "Wallet. Phone. Keys. Sunglasses..."

The effect of Pointing-and-Calling is to lift our awareness from the unconscious to the conscious. Coordinating our voice with our eyes and hands requires conscious concentration and makes us less likely to make mindless mistakes. To help apply this technique to our everyday lives, Clear comes up with an exercise called the Habits Scorecard (p. 58). It's a simple system of listing your daily habits and then categorizing them as good, bad, or neutral.

For example, a snippet of the list might look like this:

- get home from work
- chuck my coat and briefcase on the floor
- change into comfortable clothes
- take a piece of fruit from the fruit bowl
- sit on the sofa
- switch on the TV

Then, Clear asks you to put a sign next to each habit: "+" for good, "-" for bad, and "=" for neutral. Now your list will look like this:

- get home from work =
- chuck my coat and briefcase on the floor -
- change into comfortable clothes =
- take a piece of fruit from the fruit bowl +
- sit on the sofa =
- switch on the TV -

Of course, how you categorize your habits will depend on what you're trying to achieve. If you're trying not to overwork so much and take time for yourself, changing into comfortable clothes and sitting on the sofa might be a "+." But if you're trying to improve your fitness, this might not be such a good idea.

At this point, Clear makes the very good point that you should be wary of labeling your habits as "good" or "bad." It is much better to think about whether a habit serves you well in the long run or not. Similar to the exercise you did in Chapter 2, ask yourself what type of person you want to become and whether your habits vote for or against that identity. If they are for, they are helpful; if they are against, they are unhelpful.

You can take this a step further and apply the Pointing-and-Calling technique more literally. Speak the habit out loud and detail how it will benefit you, e.g., "I should go for a walk because I will feel less anxious and more healthy afterward." Or, conversely, "I am thinking about getting a McDonald's for dinner, but eating it will cause me to feel tired and gain weight, making me feel guilty." Verbalizing the consequences will make them feel more real. Suddenly, you are conscious of your actions.

Key Takeaways

- Our brain can notice a cue and start a habit without us thinking consciously about it.
- The more we pick up on cues unconsciously, the more our habits become automatic and we stop paying attention to our behavior.
- The first step towards behavior change is awareness. You cannot change a habit if you are unaware of it.
- Pointing-and-Calling and the Habits Scorecard are two useful strategies for becoming more conscious of your behavior.

Over to You

Using the example given in the summary to help you, fill in your own Habits Scorecard. Clear emphasizes that this is simply an exercise in awareness, not an action plan. The idea at this point is just to acknowledge your habits without judging yourself.

My Habits Scorecard

Daily Habits	Good (+)	Bad (-)	Neutral (=)

Chapter 5: The Best Way to Start a New Habit

Chapter Summary

Clears says that one of the most effective ways to start a new habit is to use an implementation intention (p. 62). This is a plan that specifies *where* your new habit will take place and at what *time*. This formula is effective for two key reasons: (1) it is specific, and (2) it leverages the two most common cues for the human brain: time and location. Evidence from a multitude of studies has shown that people are far more likely to follow through on their goals if they have made a specific plan for when and where to implement them.

Vague goals like "I'm going to drink less" or "I'm going to paint more" are much more difficult to fulfill because they rely on self-discipline and bursts of energy and motivation. In these cases, Clear says that the true missing ingredient is clarity. If you want to start a habit, you must make it absolutely clear what you are going to do. He creates the following formula to help with this:

"I will [BEHAVIOR] at [TIME] in [LOCATION]" (p. 64).

For instance, if you want to learn Polish, you will tell yourself, "I will study Polish for half an hour every day at 5 p.m. in my bedroom." If you want to improve your relationship with your mother, you could say, "I will call my mom at 8 p.m. on the sofa in the living room on Wednesdays, Fridays, and Saturdays." Clear's top tip here is to start your habit at the beginning of the week or month. Psychologically, these days carry more hope and motivation.

The other benefit of implementation intentions is that they make it harder to give in to tempting distractions. If you are clear about what you are going to do and how, things that are not conducive to your goal will become more apparent.

Another effective way to start a new habit is what Clear calls "habit stacking." A personal favorite of his, he credits the original method to Stanford professor BJ Fogg (p. 66). Habit stacking takes advantage of the fact that all human behavior is connected. Feeling hungry leads to opening the fridge, which reminds you that you need to buy milk, which prompts you to phone your partner and ask them to stop at the supermarket on their way home, etc. It is a strategy that builds on the implementation intention formula, only now you are associating your new habit with an already established one and not a time and location. The formula is:

"After [CURRENT HABIT], I will [NEW HABIT]" (p. 66).

For instance, if you want to practice gratitude more, you could say, "After I get into bed, I will list three things that happened that day for which I'm grateful." If you want to be better informed about current affairs, you might tell yourself, "After I make my tea in the morning, I will read one news article." The idea is to encourage the new habit to become as natural and engrained as the old one. Once you have successfully cemented one new habit, you can continue stacking more on top until it looks something like this:

1. After I make my tea in the morning, I will read one news article.

2. After I've read one news article, I will lay out my workout clothes on the sofa, ready for when I get home later.

3. After I've laid out my workout clothes, I will have a cold shower and get ready for work.

Your evening habit stack could then start with something like, "After I get home from work, I will see my workout clothes on the sofa, put them on, and go straight out for a run." Note that this is drawing on both the First and Third Laws: making it obvious and making it easy.

If you want to create a habit stack, it's important to choose an appropriate cue to trigger the chain reaction; otherwise, you're going to make things unnecessarily difficult for yourself. For example, it's no use trying to make time for reading in the morning if you have to leave very early for a long commute. Similarly, if you want to start meditating every day but you stack it onto a habit that only happens at the weekends, you're going to get stuck pretty quickly. Consider the time, place, and frequency before you start.

The strategies in this chapter provide practical ways to implement the First Law of Behavior Change: Make it obvious.

Key Takeaways

- In order for a cue to be effective it must be specific. Time and location are two of the most common examples. Avoid vague goals or statements.
- An implementation intention is a plan that specifies where your new habit will take place and at what time. The formula is: "I will [BEHAVIOR] at [TIME] in [LOCATION]."
- Habit stacking is when you attach a new habit to a current one. The formula is: "After [CURRENT HABIT], I will [NEW HABIT]."

- The First Law of Behavior Change is to make it obvious (p. 70).

Over to You

Think about what habits you would like to start. Fill in your own implementation intentions below. You can repeat this for as many habits as you like. For example:

I will go for a 20-minute run at 7 a.m. every Tuesday in the park.

Or,

I will read for 30 minutes at 10:30 p.m. every day in bed.

I will ____________________ at __________ in ________________.

I will ____________________ at __________ in ________________.

I will ____________________ at __________ in ________________.

I will ____________________ at __________ in ________________.

I will ____________________ at __________ in ________________.

If you would prefer to create a habit stack, complete the following exercise. You are welcome to use both strategies and see which one works better for you.

First, you have to pick the right cue to kickstart your habit stack. A good cue can be any daily habit or occurrence, as long as it happens consistently every day. Clear comes up with a useful exercise to help with this:

1. In the first column in the table below, list all of the habits you do every day (you should already have several lists from the previous exercises to draw from).

2. If it's easier, separate your day into morning, afternoon, and evening routines.

3. In the second column, write down everything that is guaranteed to happen to you in a day.

4. With both lists, it should now be easier to spot a good place for your new habit to slot into.

Included are a few examples to get you thinking.

Daily Habits	**Daily Happenings**
Morning	*Morning*
Check my phone. Open the fridge.	My dog comes to wake me up. My alarm goes off.

Afternoon	*Afternoon*
Make myself lunch. Take the dog for a walk.	The newspaper sends me a daily quote.
Evening	*Evening*
Go to the gym. Watch the news.	The sun sets.

It is important to list habits you do every day without fail. The more stable a habit is, the more successful you will be at attaching a new habit to it. Once you've done this, you can complete the formulas below for any new habits you wish to stack. For example:

After I work out, I will stretch for 20 minutes.

Or,

After I open the fridge, I will drink some water.

After ______________________________, I will ______________________________.

After ______________________________, I will ______________________________.

After ______________________________, I will ______________________________.

After ______________________________, I will ______________________________.

After ______________________________, I will ______________________________.

Chapter 6: Motivation Is Overrated: Environment Often Matters More

Chapter Summary

In this chapter, Clear focuses on the environment that surrounds us and how it is a key player in the First Law: make it obvious. How we behave depends heavily on the context we are in. When we are in a museum, we speak in low voices. When we are in a football stadium, we shout. Moreover, the way an environment is laid out shapes our behavior. Clear gives several examples of how big brands exploit this by strategically placing their products at eye level or in easily reachable locations. This spans from small shops and supermarkets to the urban layout of cities. We think we're choosing to go to Starbucks, but actually it's because there is one on every street corner. It's the most obvious option.

To understand why humans opt for the obvious, we must consider the priority our brains give to sight. It is by far the most powerful sense, as demonstrated by the fact that over 90 percent of our sensory receptors are dedicated to vision. It follows, then, that visual cues are the most effective for triggering human behavior. Clear explains that we can harness this fact and design our environments to be full of helpful visual cues. For the same reason, we must remove any visual cues that encourage bad habits.

It's as simple as this: if you want to eat more fruit, place a fruit bowl in the middle of your kitchen table and fill it up. If you want to practice the piano more, take all the books off it, open the lid, and place sheet music ready on the stand. Litter your environment with visual reminders of your desired habit. The more you see it, the more likely you are to do it. This last statement also applies to bad habits. If you want to game less, hide your controller on the top shelf of the cupboard. If you want to consume fewer fizzy drinks, store them at the back of the fridge behind the vegetables, or don't bring them into your house at all.

These cues can be specific to begin with. A fruit bowl. An open keyboard. Gradually, however, your habits will become associated with the location in which you practice them. The kitchen is now a place where you eat fruit. The living room is where you practice music. As Clear says, "the context becomes the cue" (p. 80).

Clear also says it can be useful to think of your environment as filled with relationships instead of objects. Consider how you interact with the items in each room and what they mean to you. This differs from person to person; a desk can be a workspace for one person and a drawing station for another. This strong association with certain objects can be difficult to shake, which is why Clear advises his readers to start a new habit in a new environment.

Think of it as a clean slate. It's no use trying to start an exercise regime in your bedroom, where all the old cues are telling you to scroll on your phone or watch Netflix in bed. Assign your habit a new space where there are no mixed signals. If you don't have much space to start with, get creative. Restructure your room to free up a corner you've never used before, or, allocate each electronic device a specific use; phone for work, iPad for leisure, etc. Clear has a mantra for this: "one space, one use" (p. 78). When the purpose of an environment is clear, your associated habit will thrive.

Key Takeaways

- Vision is our most powerful sense. Cues that stand out visually are therefore the most effective for triggering human behavior.
- Design an environment that exposes you to helpful cues and distances you from harmful ones. Bear in mind that a single habit can have multiple cues and this can make it more persistent.
- Small changes to your environment can lead to big changes in your behavior.
- Start your new habit in an environment free of already existing associations. That habit will gradually become associated with that context.
- If it is not possible to find a completely new environment, declutter and restructure the space you have available to you. Allocate a separate portion of the space to each new habit.

Over to You

The following exercise is designed to help you get a better sense of the relationships you form with your surroundings.

Come up with different types of environments that apply to you. In the first column, name five objects you have in each of those environments. In the second column, describe your relationship with those objects. It may be positive or negative, or even a mixture of both. See the examples.

Environment	Objects (or cues)	Relationship with those Objects
My bedroom.	My bed.	The place where I sleep and sometimes read or watch Netflix.
	My laptop.	The device I use to work on.
	My mirror.	Where I look at myself and sometimes feel happy with what I see, and other times not.
	My picture frames.	How I am reminded of loved ones and happy memories.
	My phone.	I check social media and WhatsApp every time my phone buzzes.
The local bar.	People drinking.	I drink with them and have fun.

Now consider the new habits you want to start or the old habits you want to break. How many of the above environments contain competing cues that will distract you from your desired behavior? This doesn't necessarily mean they're bad; they're just counterproductive to your goals. Can you come up with some brand-new environments you could use instead? How can you restructure and redefine your environments or spaces to accommodate your new habits? A few examples are given to help you.

New Habit	**New Environment or Space**
Read for an hour.	Read in the coffee shop at the local library. If you read before bed, use an armchair specifically for reading.
Buy less junk food.	Shop in a different supermarket.
Have fun without drinking.	Go to an alcohol-free bar.
Stop watching Netflix during working hours.	Only use your laptop/desktop computer specifically for work.

Hopefully these exercises will have left you with a better idea of how you interact with your surroundings. Now you can start to redesign your environment to suit the kind of behavior you aspire to. Practice filling the space with cues that make your habit more obvious. Leave a book on the bed to remind you to read before sleeping. Place bottles of water around the house to ensure that you drink more. As Clear says, “be the designer of your world and not merely the consumer of it” (p. 77).

Chapter 7: The Secret to Self-Control

Chapter Summary

The first thing Clear mentions about self-control is that it is misunderstood. The prevailing belief in Western society is that if you have bad habits, it's because you lack discipline and a moral backbone. Underpinning this is a deep-rooted culture of blame and shame.

The latest research into self-control, however, has revealed evidence that contradicts these conventional beliefs. Scientists found no significant difference in the personalities of people who seemingly had a lot of self-control and those who didn't. The real distinction came from the environments they surrounded themselves with. Those with the most self-control had designed their environment in a way that seldom required a need for it. On the other hand, those who were struggling with self-control were constantly putting themselves in situations that tested their discipline and willpower. The results created somewhat of a paradox; the less you need to use self-control, the more of it you'll have.

The problem is that, ultimately, bad habits are incredibly hard to shake. They are ingeniously designed to ensure their own survival. If you feel bad about yourself, you eat chocolate. After eating chocolate, you feel bad about yourself. And so the vicious cycle continues. Once your brain has connected chocolate with the reward of comfort and satisfaction, it will crave it compulsively every time you see it. This is known as "cue-induced wanting" (p. 83).

Clear says that the power of "cue-induced wanting" means it is almost impossible to completely forget a bad habit. You may be able to kick it, but your old patterns of behavior will remain dormant in your brain. Therefore, the most effective way to keep them from resurfacing is to remove all cues from your environment that could trigger a relapse. For example, if you're spending too much time on social media, delete the apps on your phone. If you're not using your bicycle enough, give your car keys to your partner. This method inverts Clear's First Law because now, instead of making our habits obvious, we want to make them invisible.

Key Takeaways

- People with self-control have optimized their environment to reduce exposure to temptation.
- Bad habits feed themselves. Once formed, they are very difficult to break and almost impossible to forget, especially if the environmental cues keep reappearing.
- The most effective way to avoid a bad habit is to remove all the cues that trigger it.
- When you invert the First Law of Behavior Change, you get: Make it invisible (p. 84).

Over to You

Now that we know self-control is about our environment and not a lack of will, go back to the first exercise from Chapter 6 and review the list of relationships you wrote down. Highlight any of the objects or cues that trigger undesired behavior.

For example:

Environment	**Objects (or cues)**	**Relationship with those Objects**
My bedroom.	My bed.	The place where I sleep and sometimes read or watch Netflix.
	My laptop.	The device I use to work on.
	My mirror.	Where I look at myself and sometimes feel happy with what I see, **and other times not.**
	My picture frames.	How I am reminded of loved ones and happy memories.
	My phone.	**I check social media** and WhatsApp every time my phone buzzes.

In this case, the mirror is the cue, and feeling unhappy with how you look is the bad habit. How could you optimize your environment to help you eliminate this behavior? Answer: store your mirror in the cupboard so that you're not tempted to keep looking at yourself. Concentrate on how you feel inside instead.

Make a list of all these negative cues in the table below. Brainstorm some solutions, thinking specifically about the nature of the bad habit and what changes in your environment could help you prevent it. A first example is included.

Negative cue	**Solution**
My phone (specifically, the negative cue is the notifications).	Go to settings and deactivate my notifications for WhatsApp and Instagram. Tell my friends and family to call or text me if they need to get in contact urgently.

Second Law: Make It Attractive

Chapter 8: How to Make a Habit Irresistible

Chapter Summary

In this chapter, Clear introduces the concept of "supernormal stimuli" (p. 88). This refers to cues that have been exaggerated beyond their natural limit so as to elicit an extreme reaction from your brain. He uses the example of junk food. The reason junk food is so addictive is because of the exaggerated levels of sugar and salt it contains. Our brains have evolved to think of such food as a precious commodity, having spent most of history scavenging in the wild. Although in the modern world this is no longer necessary, our systems haven't caught up yet. Hence, things like junk food still send our brains into overdrive, and our natural instinct is to eat as much as we can.

This example reveals an important lesson. If you want to make a habit stick, make it seem as attractive as possible. This is Clear's Second Law of Behavior Change (p. 89). To fully understand this point, we must first appreciate the role of dopamine in the habit formation process.

In the past, scientists thought that dopamine was solely related to pleasure. After a series of experiments in the 1950s, however, it was discovered that dopamine is also the driving force behind our motivation to act. Here's why: When we perform a habit that gives us pleasure, dopamine is released upon getting the reward.

The next time we spot the same cue, our brain skips a step and releases dopamine in anticipation of the reward, prompting a strong desire to follow through.

Indeed, studies have shown that dopamine spikes most during the craving stage of the habit cycle. This is why your habit has to be attractive. The more desirable the reward, the more dopamine your brain will release and the more motivated you'll feel to act.

The importance of the Second Law is further supported by the fact that the "wanting centers" of the brain are much larger than the "liking centers" (p. 93). The region of the brain concerned with motivation and action—the nucleus accumbens—is activated 100 percent when we want something, but only 10 percent when we like something. Clear presents us with all of this evidence to drive home a key message: To build a successful habit, you must harness the power of anticipation and use it to make the habit seem irresistible.

One of the best techniques for employing this strategy is "temptation bundling" (p. 93). This is when you pair up a habit that you *want* to do with one that you *need* to do. For instance, if you love listening to music but need to get better at tidying up, you could only play music while you're cleaning the house. Similarly, if you want to surf through Instagram but you need to practice your French, you could change the language settings on your social media account to French only. Clear lays out a formula for this, which he gets by combining temptation bundling with his habit stacking technique from Chapter 5.

1. "After [CURRENT HABIT], I will [HABIT I NEED]."
2. "After [HABIT I NEED], I will [HABIT I WANT]" (p. 95).

For example, if you want to have a bath but are trying to build a habit of gardening regularly:

1. After I hang my coat up, I will do one hour of weeding in the garden (NEED).
2. After I've done one hour of weeding in the garden, I will take a bath (WANT).

Over time, you'll begin to associate the habit you need to develop with getting to do something you really enjoy, and the whole idea of it will become more attractive. You might even start to look forward to it.

Key Takeaways

- Dopamine is the force that drives the habit cycle. It incentivizes the cue by associating it with the reward. Without dopamine, we do not feel the desire or motivation to act.
- Every highly habit-forming behavior is associated with higher levels of dopamine. Drug addiction is a prime example of this.
- We are more likely to do something if we anticipate a reward. Making a habit as attractive as possible will increase anticipation, which in turn will optimize dopamine levels.
- Temptation bundling is when you combine what you *want* to do with what you *need* to do.
- The Second Law of Behavior Change is to make it attractive (p. 96).

Over to You

In the table below, identify three cravings you have, what triggers them (cue), and why. If it helps, write the craving down first (in the middle column) and then fill in either side. See the examples given first.

Cue	**Craving**	**Why**
Spotting my gym mat.	I want to stretch after work.	I feel very relaxed afterward.
I see my boyfriend/girlfriend.	I want to hug my boyfriend/girlfriend.	Physical touch makes me feel more loved and releases oxytocin.
I come across an article about psychology.	I want to read that article.	So I can share interesting insights with other people and win their respect and approval.

Cue	**Craving**	**Why**

Cravings are essentially things you want to do. Including the three you just listed above, write down all of the things you enjoy doing in the first column below. In the next column, write down all of the things you need to do but don't feel motivated to do. Order does not matter. See some examples.

Things I want to do	Things I need to do
I want to read psychology articles.	I need to take out the trash.
I want to hug my boyfriend/girlfriend.	I need to drink more water.
I want to stretch after work.	I need to meditate more.

See if any of the activities on either list could feasibly be paired up with each other. For example:

"For every page I read in my psychology magazine, I will take one big sip of water."

You can then take it a step further and combine it with the habit stacking technique. To use a different example:

1. After I get home from work, I will meditate for 10 minutes (NEED).
2. After I meditate for 10 minutes, I will join my boyfriend/girlfriend on the sofa and give them a hug (WANT).

Use the two lists of activities to write out your own temptation bundles below. Use the habit stacking add-on to make your goals even more precise. Here is the formula to remind you:

1. "After [CURRENT HABIT], I will [HABIT I NEED]."
2. "After [HABIT I NEED], I will [HABIT I WANT]."

#1

After ______________________________, I will ____________________________.

After ______________________________, I will ____________________________.

#2

After ______________________________, I will ____________________________.

After ______________________________, I will ____________________________.

#3

After ____________________________, I will ____________________________.

After ____________________________, I will ____________________________.

#4

After ____________________________, I will ____________________________.

After ____________________________, I will ____________________________.

#5

After ____________________________, I will ____________________________.

After ____________________________, I will ____________________________.

Now that you have laid out a clear plan, you should hopefully feel more confident about tackling these goals. Try putting some of them into action!

Chapter 9: The Role of Family and Friends in Shaping Your Habits

Chapter Summary

Humans are social creatures. We are constantly looking for ways to fit in and be accepted by our tribe. In the past, this was an evolutionary necessity. We had to collaborate to survive. In the modern world, this conditioning continues to play a key role in how we behave, and nothing demonstrates this desire to belong more than how we form our habits.

Our behavior is a reflection of the social and cultural norms that we live in. The family we're born into, the neighborhood we grow up in, what school we go to, which friends we make, etc.—all of these factors influence how we think and act. We imitate the habits of those around us because we want to feel like we belong. Clear highlights three groups that have a particular influence in this regard; the close, the many, and the powerful (p. 99).

The Close

It goes without saying that the people closest to us are the ones whose behavior we are exposed to the most. As a result, we quickly pick up their habits. We imitate the body language of our parents, the slang words of our friends, and the problem-solving skills of our colleagues. Often, we do this without even realizing it.

One of the best ways to make your habit more attractive, then, is to join a club or society that focuses on that habit. That way, your desired behavior becomes not only the norm but also regularly practiced. For example, if you join a cycling group, you'll soon come to think that cycling for miles every weekend is normal. Or, if you sign up for a book club, you'll quickly get into the rhythm of reading two books a month.

Building a new habit will feel far more achievable if you are surrounded by like-minded people who already practice and enjoy that habit. That way, your goal will become less of a lonely effort and more of an act of joining in—something we humans love to do anyway.

The Many

We are constantly looking to the majority for confirmation and validation. The more people who agree, the more likely we are to believe it. Actions like checking for the best reviews or reading comments on feedback forums are prime examples of this.

Clear notes that conforming to the group is not always the best option. The desire to fit in can sometimes go against our better judgment. For example, if one person knows a shortcut to a restaurant but the rest of their group has already started down a much longer route, they will most likely just go along with the group rather than make a fuss. As Clear says, "most days, we'd rather be wrong with the crowd than be right by ourselves" (p. 103).

Building a new habit that challenges the majority is therefore going to make things unnecessarily difficult for you. Make it more attractive by aligning your desired behavior with that of the group.

The Powerful

Humans are naturally attracted to power and success. Once we've spent all that energy and effort fitting in with the crowd, our next desire is to stand out. It follows, then, that we imitate the behavior of the people who impress us most. This could be dressing like your favorite celebrity or watching TED talks given by your business idol. We crave other people's respect and approval, so building a habit that gets us similar attention is highly attractive. Clear notes that this works the other way too; we avoid behavior that brings us scorn or disapproval.

To make your habit as attractive as possible, then, ensure that it's valued by the culture that surrounds you. The more praise you receive, the more reason you'll have to stick with it, and the better chance your habit will have of lasting.

Key Takeaways

- We are a product of the culture we live in; our behavior reflects the norms of that culture.
- We imitate the habits of those around us in order to fit in. Three groups that have a particular influence over us are: the close, the many, and the powerful.
- One of the best ways to build a habit and maintain it is to join a group of like-minded people who already practice and enjoy that habit.
- Our desire to be accepted means that we conform to a group even when it goes against our better judgment. Your habit will require less effort if it aligns with the behavior and beliefs of your group.
- A habit will be more attractive to us if it leads to respect and approval.

Over to You

Think about some of your habits, past or current, good and bad. Where did they come from? Did your friend tell you about it? Did you read it online? Were you put up to it by your parents? As a quick exercise, jot down some examples of habits that were inspired by Clear's three social groups: the close, the many, and the powerful. After the first example, write two to three for each category.

The Close	**The Many**	**The Powerful**
Habit: Tennis club. Origin: I started going to tennis class every Thursday because my best friend was already going.	Habit: Putting cinnamon in my water in the morning. Origin: I saw a video posted online by a health blogger saying that adding cinnamon to your water boosts your metabolism. It was the video with the most likes.	Habit: Playing the piano. Origin: My parents put me in classes when I was six, and I enjoyed the praise I got from them and my teacher as I moved up the grades.

Reflecting on the origins of your habits is useful because it reveals what you find attractive in a habit. Knowing what impresses and motivates you gives you an excellent clue as to what needs to be done to start a new habit. In the table below, think about how you could leverage Clear's three social groups to make your new habits more attractive. A first example has been given to get you started.

Desired Habit	**How do I make it more attractive?**	**Which group does this leverage?**
To spend more time in nature.	Become a member of a local wildlife trust. They organize weekly nature walks and give you exclusive access to rewilding projects.	The Close.

Chapter 10: How to Find and Fix the Causes of Your Bad Habits

Chapter Summary

In this chapter, Clear looks at what happens when you invert the Second Law: make it unattractive. He starts by going back to cravings. He says that underlying all of our cravings are a set of core, instinctual motives. These include but are not limited to: eating and drinking to survive, experiencing love and connection, reproducing, seeking acceptance and status in a tribe, and overcoming uncertainty.

Clear maintains that any craving can be traced back to these deep-rooted motives, no matter how specific or modern. Drinking alcohol is a manifestation of seeking acceptance or reducing stress and anxiety. Going to the hairdresser is about winning approval and potentially attracting a mate. Habits are therefore the solutions we come up with in response to these perennial desires and problems.

These solutions can manifest in many different ways. For example, you may have learned to manage your anxiety by smoking. But someone else might manage their anxiety by practicing meditation, going for long walks, or meeting up with friends. Whatever the solution is, if it is successful in satisfying the underlying motive, your brain will remember it for next time.

In other words, if the habit is attractive, your brain will develop a craving for it. The key to breaking a bad habit, therefore, is to make it unattractive. Clear reminds his readers here that craving something simply means wanting a change. You smoke to feel less stressed, but it is the change in state that you crave, not the cigarette itself. Your brain has just learned to associate smoking cigarettes with the solution to the problem.

The first step, then, is to change your mindset. Reframe this association you have with smoking—to continue the previous example—by highlighting everything you have to gain by avoiding it. For instance, you will greatly improve your health and physical appearance, you will save a lot of money, you won't feel so on edge and desperate, etc. After a while, smoking will only carry negative associations, and our brains will decide the behavior is not worth repeating. The habit will become unattractive.

Conversely, by associating difficult habits with positive experiences, we can make them seem more attractive. Clear uses the simple but powerful example of replacing one word in a sentence. Instead of saying, "I *have* to pick up the kids," tell yourself, "I *get* to pick up the kids." Similarly, "I *have* to do the food shopping" becomes "I *get* to do the food shopping." By shifting your perspective, you have turned these tedious tasks into opportunities, thus making them more appealing.

Furthermore, if a habit requires a lot of effort, put a positive spin on things and focus on the benefits. For example, if you need to go to the gym before work, tell yourself, "My fitness will improve, and I will be invigorated for the day." If you need to tend to your garden, say to yourself, "I will get lots of fresh air, and the view from my kitchen will be much prettier." It might not seem like much, but these changes in mindset can help create a positive association with your habit and make it more likely that you'll do it.

Clear says you can take this a step further and create "a motivation ritual" (p. 112). This is when you precede a difficult habit with an activity you enjoy doing. For instance, listening to music before doing the dishes, or closing your eyes and thinking of your favorite place before giving a presentation at work. The idea is that once you've repeated it enough times, you will come to associate these habits with enjoyable experiences. The cue of turning on the stereo will motivate you to wash up. The cue of closing your eyes will focus your attention and calm your nerves before a presentation. These simple but effective rituals will help reprogram your brain to enjoy difficult habits.

Key Takeaways

- Underlying all of our behavior is a set of core, instinctual motives. They are all linked to survival.
- We form habits in response to these underlying motives. Identifying the motive behind the behavior can therefore help us to exchange bad habits for good ones.
- Two people can come up with very different habits to deal with the same motive.
- The key to avoiding bad habits and enjoying difficult ones is to change your mindset.
- Create a motivation ritual to associate a difficult habit with a positive experience. This will make it more attractive.
- Make the unattractive qualities of bad habits obvious by highlighting everything you have to gain by avoiding them.
- When you invert the Second Law of Behavior Change, you get: Make it unattractive (p. 113).

Over to You

In the table below, list three habits you are trying to avoid. Think about why you do them—what core, instinctual motives are behind each one? Understanding this will help you get to the root of the problem and find creative alternatives. Then, in the final column, list the benefits you seek to gain by avoiding them. This will hopefully make the habits seem much less attractive. See the example.

Habit I want to avoid	**Underlying motives behind it**	**Benefits I gain from avoiding it**
Biting my fingernails.	Relieves stress. Overcomes boredom. Self-grooming.	I will not be in pain. My hands won't look raw and bloody. I'll attract less attention and concern from people.

Now do a similar exercise with three habits that you have been putting off. Put a positive spin on them by thinking about all the benefits they have to offer.

If you want to push yourself, see if you can come up with a motivation ritual for each one. See the example.

Difficult Habits	**Benefits Gained**	**Motivation Ritual**
Going for a run in the morning.	I will feel energized for the rest of the day. I will improve my health and fitness. I will get fresh air. I can explore different areas where I live.	After I wake up, I will play my favorite song as I put on my running clothes. Just before I open the front door, I will clap my hands together and say out loud, "You've got this!"

Third Law: Make It Easy

Chapter 11: Walk Slowly, but Never Backward

Chapter Summary

When we want to implement change, we often get caught up in searching for the best option or the perfect plan. But Clear says this is counterproductive to our goals. He notes that people spend so much time preparing for change that they never actually get around to doing anything. He calls this "the difference between being in motion and taking action" (p. 117).

The two things can feel very similar. If you've come up with a plan for where and when to start playing the guitar, for example, it can feel very productive. You may have even gone out and bought a new one. But you're still just in motion at this point; you haven't actually produced any results. Sitting down and physically practicing is the only way you'll learn how to play. This is taking action.

This is not to say that preparation isn't useful. As we have seen in the previous chapters, laying out a clear plan will certainly help deliver results. Clear's point here is to not let motion turn into procrastination. The way to do this is to focus on repeating a habit, not perfecting it. This is a feature of the Third Law of Behavior Change: Make it easy.

Here we are introduced to a concept called "automaticity" (p. 119). It refers to the process through which a habit becomes automatic. As we saw in Chapter 3, habits are formed through a process of repetition. The more we repeat a behavior, the stronger the neural pathways for that activity become. Eventually, we get to a point where the behavior feels effortless and we can do it without thinking. This indicates that we have crossed the threshold of conscious engagement, or what Clear calls "the habit line" (p. 119).

Essentially, if you want to get better at something, you have to do it lots of times. Crossing the habit line is a matter of repetition, not time. It's no good saying you've been playing the guitar for three months if you only practiced a handful of times during that period. You will improve much faster within a week if you practice twice a day. This is Clear's key message of the chapter: when it comes to forming a habit, frequency is more important than length of time.

Key Takeaways

- Preparation and planning give us the impression that we're making progress but don't actually deliver results; taking action does.
- The key to habit formation is repetition.
- The frequency with which you practice a habit is more important than the length of time you've been doing it.
- The Third Law of Behavior Change is to make it easy (p. 121).

Over to You

Before you start the next exercise, just take a moment to reflect on a habit that you have tried to start but failed to do in the past.

Why do you think it failed? Did you spend too much time on the planning stage and not enough on the action? Or, conversely, did you dive straight into the action and not think it through? Perhaps it was due to a lack of motivation—did you give it a chance and repeat it enough times?

Now think about a habit that was successful. How was this time different? What did you get right?

On a separate piece of paper, draw a graph. This is for you to track the progress of your new habit. Label the vertical axis 'automaticity' and number it from 1 to 10, 1 being the least automatic and 10 being fully automatic. Label the horizontal axis "days." How many days you decide to track is up to you, but around 100 should be adequate. To see an example, you can go to page 120 of Clear's book.

Every time you repeat your desired behavior, mark an "X" on the graph according to the day and how automatic it felt. Naturally, your Xs will start off low on the automaticity scale. The more you repeat the behavior, the higher the Xs will climb. If you are unsure about your progress, ask yourself, "How much did I consciously have to think about that?"

What you should get is an upwards curve. With enough repetitions, this curve will begin to even out. This is an indication that your behavior has crossed the habit line and become automatic (when it has reached or is close to 10).

Chapter 12: The Law of Least Effort

Chapter Summary

Humans have evolved to follow the Law of Least Effort (p. 124). This refers to the fact that, when making decisions, we usually opt for the easy, most convenient path. Rather than dismiss it as lazy, Clear says this is a highly efficient strategy because it allows us to conserve our energy. He advises his readers to take it into account when they are forming new habits.

In other words, if your habit requires a lot of energy up front, it is going to be met with more resistance. For example, if you set a goal of swimming 70 laps a day, you are demanding a lot from your body. You will quickly tire after a couple of days, and it is unlikely that you will continue. Swimming five laps a day, on the other hand, is much more doable. The less effort your habit requires, the more successful it will be. Think of all the most common habits, such as watching television, eating ice-cream, or scrolling through Instagram. They enjoy such high levels of success because they require little to no effort.

Clear says to think of a habit as an obstacle that is standing between you and the final outcome. Running is an obstacle to losing weight. Tidying up is an obstacle to feeling relaxed. If you can reduce the size and weight of the obstacle—i.e., make the habit as convenient as possible—you will find it much easier to achieve your desired outcome. He refers to this generally as "reducing friction."

An effective way to reduce friction is to work on your environment. We covered this in Chapter 6 when we talked about making cues obvious. Now, we can build on that by using environment design to make our desired behavior easy to do.

Consider first where your new habit will take place. Pick a location that is easily accessible and, preferably, already part of your daily routine. For example, you might want to start a rollerblading habit. If you walk past a large open space every day on your way to work, you could bring the rollerblades in your bag and practice on the way home. This way, your new habit introduces as little friction to your life as possible.

Consider also the nature of your environment. If it already contains a lot of friction, your habit will be harder to start. For instance, if you try to practice meditation in your living room when everyone else is arriving home, it's going to be distracting and chaotic. Similarly, if you try to go for a run on the weekend, the streets are going to be busy with cars and people.

Clear uses a strategy he calls "addition by subtraction" to tackle this (p. 126). It refers to the systematic removal of all sources of friction in your environment. You subtract friction to add time, energy, and space. Companies all over the world employ this strategy in a continuous race to produce the easiest-to-use product. Machines are becoming increasingly automated, apps constantly minimalized, forms evermore simplified.

Clear further notes that setting up your space for future use is a very handy way to keep good habits easy and convenient. It means that when you come to that action, there is barely any friction to get through. For example, if you want to eat healthier lunches, lay out two pieces of fruit and a bottle of water on the kitchen counter the night before. The next morning, it'll be easy to pack them into your lunchbox.

This also works the other way around. Increasing the friction around your bad habits will help to deter you from them. For instance, if you want to work at home without any distractions, leave your phone in the other room. That will create enough friction to ensure that you don't go get it unless you really need it.

If you want to take more drastic measures, you could also delete your social media apps or ask a partner or friend to change the password on your account.

Priming our environment in this way can make a big difference in how easy it is to stick to good habits and how hard it is to repeat bad ones.

Key Takeaways

- The Law of Least Effort says that humans naturally opt for the easy, most convenient path when making decisions.
- If a habit requires a lot of effort, it is less likely to be successful.
- If a habit requires little effort, it is more likely to be successful. Try to make your good habits fit into the flow of your daily life.
- "Addition by subtraction" is Clear's technique for removing friction in your environment.
- Make good habits easier by reducing friction and bad habits harder by increasing friction.
- Setting up your space for future use is a very handy way to keep good habits easy and convenient.

Over to You

Following Clear's concept of "addition by subtraction," think about how you could organize your environment to reduce the friction of each desired habit. The aim here is to make them as easy as possible. A first example has been given for you.

Ways to reduce friction	**How this will make my good habits easier**
Before I go to bed, I will place my vitamins on the kitchen counter.	This will remind me to take my vitamins, as they will be the first thing I see when I come down for breakfast.

Now invert this strategy and list a few examples of how you could increase the friction in your environment to help avoid bad habits.

Ways to increase friction	**How this will make my bad habits harder**
I will ask my taller partner to put all of the sweets and chocolate on the very top shelf in the kitchen.	The sweets and chocolate will now be out of reach and sight. I will only be able to get them if I pull up a chair or ask my partner to get them for me.

Chapter 13: How to Stop Procrastinating by Using the Two-Minute Rule

Chapter Summary

A habit might only take a few seconds to complete, but it can have a lasting effect on your day. Clear uses an example from his own life to demonstrate this. If he collapses onto the sofa after work, he will order takeout and watch TV. If he changes into his workout clothes straight after work, he will go to the gym. One unconscious decision can set you down a certain path and determine what your subsequent behavior will be without you even knowing it. Clear calls these choices "decisive moments" (p. 132).

Decisive moments can be the difference between encouraging a good habit and slipping into a bad one. So as not to be limited by them, Clear says it is important to be aware of these moments and to master them.

This is where he introduces the main focus of the chapter, a technique he calls "the Two-Minute Rule" (p. 134). Clear came up with this rule in response to so many people overdoing it when they first start a habit. It's very tempting to make big changes at the beginning when you're full of excitement and motivation. But instead, you should start small. Limit your new habit to a two-minute version.

For instance, a running habit might get scaled down to putting on your shoes and opening the front door. A reading habit might be scaled down to opening the book and reading the first page. The idea behind the Two-Minute Rule is to make the beginning of your habit as easy and manageable as possible. With enough repetition, these first two minutes will have a ritualizing effect, and you will find it easier to get into the zone. Once productive behavior is made easy to start, it becomes natural to follow through.

It might seem strange to only put on your running shoes or only read one page, but the point is to practice committing to your habit before you start perfecting it. As Clear says, first you must "master the habit of showing up" (p. 135). Only when this has been established can you hope to develop it.

Clear notes that the Two-Minute Rule can feel contrived for some people, so he suggests looking at it like this instead: think of those two minutes as your entire habit. You can only do whatever is achievable within this time and nothing more. For example, you can go to a nearby park and do two 10-second sprints with a 90-second rest in between. This makes a total of two minutes. Or, you can get your paper and pencils out and start drawing, but you must stop after two minutes.

By purposefully doing *less* than you feel like, your habit never becomes a burden, and you are left wanting to do more. Clear reminds his readers that this practice is also good for casting votes for your desired identity, as discussed in Chapter 2.

Once you've got your two-minute version down, you can start developing your habit using a technique Clear calls "habit shaping" (p. 136). This helps you build your habit by advancing in stages. Focus on mastering each stage—just as you did with the first two minutes—before you move on. For example, building a good sleeping habit might look something like this:

Stage 1: Stop drinking caffeine after 3 p.m.

Stage 2: Make sure you're home by 10 p.m. every night.

Stage 3: Set your alarm for 7 a.m. in the mornings, even if you went to bed late and it means you'll be tired.

Stage 4: Don't look at a screen after 10 p.m.

Stage 5: Turn off the lights and be in bed by 10:30 p.m.

Breaking your actions down into manageable stages—and, most importantly, using the first two minutes as a ritual to focus—will allow you to successfully build any habit, no matter how ambitious.

Key Takeaways

- A habit might only take a few seconds to complete, but it can have a lasting effect on your day.
- Certain habitual choices can be defined as "decisive moments;" they determine whether your subsequent behavior will be productive or unproductive.
- The Two-Minute Rule is a strategy that downsizes your habit to an action that only takes up to two minutes to complete.
- The idea behind this is to make the beginning of your habit an action that is as easy, manageable, and sustainable as possible. Once engrained, these first two minutes can then act as a ritual for getting into the zone of productive working.
- Habit shaping is when you build your habit up in stages—mastering each stage before you move on.

Over to You

The following exercise will help you find the two-minute version of your habits. First, think about what your habit would look like at various stages of difficulty. The table below follows Clear's scale, from "very easy" to "very hard" (p. 134-5). Underneath the first example, write three of your own.

Very easy	**Easy**	**Moderate**	**Hard**	**Very hard**
Open your book.	Read one page.	Read three chapters.	Finish the whole book.	Complete the trilogy.

Now look at the first column: "very easy." This version is what your habit would look like if you applied the Two-Minute Rule. To begin with, make it your goal to start practicing just that version. Once you've nailed it, you will notice a natural inclination to follow through.

If you want to take this even further, you can combine the Two-Minute Rule with Clear's "habit shaping" technique. To build on the previous example, see what developing a reading habit might look like below. Notice that it starts with the easiest versions of the habit.

Stage 1: Open your book and read the first page.

Stage 2: Make time to read at least three times a week.

Stage 3: Finish five books.

Stage 4: Sign up for a book club.

Stage 5: Read one book per month and discuss it at the book club.

Now you try:

<u>Habit #1</u>

Stage 1:

Stage 2:

Stage 3:

Stage 4:

Stage 5:

Habit #2

Stage 1:

Stage 2:

Stage 3:

Stage 4:

Stage 5:

Habit #3

Stage 1:

Stage 2:

Stage 3:

Stage 4:

Stage 5:

Habit #4

Stage 1:

Stage 2:

Stage 3:

Stage 4:

Stage 5:

Chapter 14: How to Make Good Habits Inevitable and Bad Habits Impossible

Chapter Summary

In this chapter, Clear looks at a few different ways you can make it hard for yourself to repeat bad habits. This is the main principle of the inverted Third Law of Behavior Change: Make it difficult (p. 139).

The first way is to use a "commitment device" (p. 139). This can take many different forms, but essentially, it is a method by which you control your future actions, a means to enforce good behavior. For example, installing an app on your phone that limits your screen time or paying for a gym class in advance so that you feel compelled to show up. This can be very effective, as it greatly reduces your exposure to tempting situations. As Clear says, the trick is to make falling into a bad habit *more* of a hassle than staying on track.

Even more effective is to find a way to automate good behavior. While a commitment device will make good habits more likely, automation will make them inevitable. This leads to Clear's concept of "onetime actions" (p. 141). This refers to simple actions you can take that will continue to deliver results without you ever having to think about them again. Some examples Clear gathered from his readers are: buying a more comfortable mattress to help you sleep better; swapping your plates for smaller ones in order to eat less; and getting a dog to improve your well-being.

Technology can also be a big help when it comes to automation. It is particularly useful for actions that don't occur frequently enough to be at the top of your mind, such as paying monthly bills or remembering security information. Processes that were once bothersome and complicated have become swift and painless. If you can dedicate as many tasks to technology as possible, you can spend more time enriching and improving other areas of your life.

Clear notes here that technology can also pose problems for us. After all, so many of our bad habits revolve around screen addiction and binge-watching. This is because the ease of technology has made life *too* convenient. If we're not careful, we can fall into the danger of never having to face anything difficult.

Key Takeaways

- A "commitment device" is a way for your present self to ensure that your future self abides by good behavior.
- An even more effective technique is to automate your behavior. This can be achieved through "onetime actions" which are simple, one-off decisions that will continue to deliver results in the future.
- If used properly, the surest way to automate your behavior is by using technology.
- When you invert the Third Law of Behavior Change, you get: Make it difficult (p. 144).

Over to You

Clear is confident that onetime actions are an easy way to make your life better. Think about areas of your life that could be improved by better habits. Perhaps you could do with sleeping better or eating healthier. Maybe you're not feeling productive or satisfied with your work.

In the table below, brainstorm a list of onetime actions you could take to automate better behavior. You can also enlist the help of technology and commitment devices to make these onetime actions more effective. If any of the given categories don't apply, add your own. A few examples have been given to help get you started.

Areas of Life	Onetime Actions
Eating & Drinking.	Sign up for a weekly fruit & veg box.
Sleeping.	Buy blackout blinds. Buy some oxygenating houseplants.
Waking Up Early.	Install an alarm clock that needs a QR code to be deactivated. Place the QR code on the kitchen wall.
Mental Health.	Move to a sunnier country.

Exercise.	Organize an early running date with a buddy to avoid the temptation of canceling.
Work Productivity.	Use an automated setting to filter your emails.
Phone Addiction.	Mute your notifications.
Family.	Set a weekly reminder and have your parents call you at 8 p.m. every Sunday.
Relationships.	Add all of your friends' birthdays to your calendar.

Finances.	Research and hire an experienced financial advisor.

Fourth Law: Make It Satisfying

Chapter 15: The Cardinal Rule of Behavior Change

Chapter Summary

The best way to motivate ourselves to repeat a good habit is to make it satisfying. As discussed in Chapter 8, if a habit gives us pleasure, our brain will be sure to repeat it. This leads Clear to his "Cardinal Rule of Behavior Change" (p. 149). It says that if you want a habit to be repeated, you must reward it. Conversely, if you want a habit to be avoided, you must punish it. This forms the basis of the final law: make it satisfying (p. 149).

Clear clarifies that the type of satisfaction he is talking about is immediate, not delayed. We live in a society that is referred to scientifically as a delayed-return environment (p. 150). This means that we do not see the benefits of our actions straight away, but rather receive them weeks, months, and sometimes years down the line. Our brains, however, have not yet caught up with this recent evolutionary advancement. They are still functioning on an immediate-return basis, as was necessary in the prehistoric past.

This tendency to live in the present is a smart strategy most of the time. After all, the future is speculative; we can only be certain of what is happening to us right now. However, sometimes our desire for instant gratification gets us into trouble. As Clear points out, why do we smoke if we know it can lead to cancer? Why do we have unprotected sex if we know it can give us an STD? It is because our bad habits give us greater immediate rewards. Our brains prioritize this over the consequences, which are often delayed and therefore don't concern us in the moment.

Unfortunately, the opposite is true for our good habits. The immediate outcome isn't usually very gratifying, and we have to wait a lot longer to be rewarded. When given the option, most people will choose the path of instant satisfaction. This is why individuals who practice delayed gratification are often more successful; they encounter less competition.

The good news, Clear says, is that we can use these insights to our advantage. For instance, if you want to encourage a good habit, add an immediate reward at the end. If you want to deter a bad habit, add an immediate punishment. The key is to make either engaging in or avoiding your habit as impactful as possible. Clear points out that we tend to remember the last part of an experience more than any other. This is why it is more effective to place the reward or punishment at the end of a habit. He refers to this process as "immediate reinforcement" (p. 153).

This works particularly well for what Clear calls "habits of avoidance" (p. 153). If you want to avoid buying clothes, for example, think about something that money could go towards instead—perhaps a holiday, or a new sofa. Create a separate account and put money into it every time you resist a purchase. If you saw a jacket for $100 but didn't buy it, transfer the $100 to your account instead. If you almost bought a skirt for $17, transfer $17. The satisfaction of seeing your money accumulate will make you feel better about not buying clothes. And at the end of the year, you will have a chunk of money to either go on a holiday with or buy a new sofa.

When using immediate reinforcement, Clear reminds his readers to bear in mind the type of identity they are working towards. It is important that the two don't clash. For example, if you're trying to improve your fitness, rewarding yourself with beer and pizza isn't going to help. It might be a better idea to go for a sauna or treat yourself to a massage. When you align your immediate rewards with your long-term goals, you will be even more successful.

Eventually, you will start to see the natural effects of your good habits coming through, and that will become powerful motivation in itself. With a habit of getting fit, for instance, intrinsic rewards like increased stamina and an improved mood will start to kick in, and you won't have to rely so much on extra incentives to keep you going. The habit will become self-satisfying and your new identity will sustain it.

Key Takeaways

- Good habits require effort in the present but pay off in the future. Bad habits feel good in the present but cost you in the future.
- The best way to motivate ourselves to repeat a good habit is to make it satisfying.
- Our brains function on an immediate-return basis. As a result, they will usually opt for instant satisfaction over delayed gratification, regardless of the consequences.
- If you want a habit to be repeated, you must immediately reward it. If you want a habit to be avoided, you must immediately punish it. This is Clear's Cardinal Rule of Behavior Change.

- Make sure these immediate rewards don't clash with your desired identity. This is important because it will be your identity that eventually sustains your habit.
- The Fourth Law of Behavior Change is to make it satisfying (p. 155).

Over to You

This exercise will help you put Clear's technique of immediate reinforcement into practice. First, think about how you can make your good habits more immediately enjoyable. Next, consider how to reward yourself for avoiding bad habits.

In both cases, remember to make sure the rewards you choose are aligned with your desired identity. This will ensure that your habit is sustainable. Write your ideas down in the corresponding tables. An example has been given for each.

Good Habits	Reward at the end	How does this reinforce my identity?
Learning how to cook for myself.	Every time I learn a new recipe, I will invite my friends over for a dinner party.	I want to be more mindful of the ingredients I put into my body so that I can feel more energized.

Habits of Avoidance	**Reward at the end**	**How does this reinforce my identity?**
Drinking alcohol on weekdays.	For every dollar I save by not buying drinks during the week, I will put a dollar towards my next weekend getaway.	I want to be someone who isn't held back by constant hangovers.

Chapter 16: How to Stick with Good Habits Every Day

Chapter Summary

Clear opens this chapter with an anecdote about a stockbroker who used paper clips to mark how many sales calls he made each day. He uses it to demonstrate a technique for making good habits more satisfying—one he coins "the Paper Clip Strategy" (p. 156).

This stockbroker would start every day with 120 paper clips in one jar and zero in another. Every time he made a sales call, he would move one paper clip over to the empty jar. He kept going until he had transferred all 120 of them. The point of this technique is to allow you to keep a visual track of your habit. Watching your progress accumulate is very satisfying, and it motivates you to continue.

You can use any visual means to employ this strategy; it doesn't have to be paper clips. Clear says the best way is to use what he calls a "habit tracker" (p. 157). This is a simple but effective way to keep track of your progress. For example, buy yourself a calendar and mark the days that you stick to your habit with an X. Or, get yourself a small notebook and make a note of the date each time you practice your habit. Habit tracking is so effective because it draws on several Laws of Behavior Change at once. Clear breaks it down:

Habit tracking makes it obvious

The habit tracker is a visual cue in itself. Whenever you walk into your room, you will see the calendar marked with Xs and be reminded to do your habit. Evidence from studies shows that people who keep a physical record of their progress do better than those who don't.

Recording your actions also forces you to be honest with yourself. When left to our memories, we often think that we're doing better or worse than we actually are. But we can't pretend to ourselves that we're doing well if we're staring at a blank calendar. Likewise, we have to take some credit when the record clearly shows that we've been practicing three times a week.

Habit tracking makes it attractive

There is nothing more morale-boosting than making progress. It has a seductive effect on our brains and gives us the motivation to push forward. This is especially true if you're having a bad day. It's normal to feel dispirited sometimes, but when you do, look at the evidence from your habit tracker and you will regain a sense of achievement. This will also motivate you not to slack off, as seeing gaps in your progress is unattractive.

Habit tracking makes it satisfying

Clear says this is the most important aspect of habit tracking. Being able to tick something off your list or fill out an empty square is hugely satisfying. Seeing the results multiply makes us feel good—and as we have seen, if an action gives us pleasure, we repeat it.

Habit tracking also encourages us to enjoy the process and not simply obsess over the end goal. It allows us to take joy in the small wins instead of delaying happiness. This goes back to some of the first points that Clear makes in his book: to focus on your systems and implement change on a deeper, identity-based level.

Clear says that he has delayed talking about habit tracking until now because it can put some people off. For those who are already struggling to stick to one habit, adding *another* habit of tracking your actions can seem like an unnecessary extra burden.

In answer to this, Clear says firstly to automate habit tracking as much as you can. The technology around you is already doing this more than you realize. Banking apps track our spending, phones measure our screen time, Fitbits count our footsteps, Google Maps remembers where we've traveled to, and so on. Much of the data is already there; you just need to remember to access it regularly.

Secondly, there's no need to measure everything. Don't get overwhelmed by trying to track all of your habits, just pick the most important ones—or the ones that need the most supervision. And finally, record your behavior immediately after completing it. That way, you don't have to think about it again. Clear provides a formula for this. It combines habit tracking with the habit-stacking technique we saw in Chapter 5:

"After [CURRENT HABIT], I will [TRACK MY HABIT]" (p. 160).

An example of this might look like this: "After I do 15 minutes of stretching, I will mark the day in my calendar." Or, "After I hang up the phone with my sister, I will make a note of it in my diary." All of these can be useful tactics for making habit tracking easier. If you're still not convinced, just try it for a week or two. You might be surprised at how insightful it is.

At this point, Clear reminds his readers that they won't always be able to keep up a perfect streak. Life is unpredictable. For situations like these, he has a golden rule: "Never miss twice" (p. 160). This means that it's okay to slip up once, as long as you don't repeat the mistake twice in a row. For instance, if you binge-watch a tv show one night, don't panic—just make sure you go for a walk the following evening. If you skip a yoga class, make it a priority to turn up for the next one.

Clear says this is a key difference between failure and success. Anyone can have an off day; it is how quickly you bounce back that matters. In fact, not breaking the chain is so important that you should show up even when you don't have the energy to do the habit well. Clear is adamant about this. Bad days are far better than no-shows. And besides, you want to cast votes for the type of person who shows up no matter what. Having an all-or-nothing attitude is the fastest way to derail your habits.

Clear ends this chapter with a warning. When it comes to habit tracking, be careful not to get obsessed with the numbers. It is only a useful technique as long as it facilitates the original purpose of the habit. For example, if you care more about reaching a certain weight on the scale than feeling happy and energized, you have lost sight of the original reason for eating healthier.

In a world that places too much value on numbers, we mustn't forget about all the unquantifiable factors. Just because you can measure your weight on a scale doesn't mean that it's the best way to monitor your progress. Why not track how healthy your skin looks instead? Or how much your mood has improved? Measuring progress is a super useful and satisfying tool, as long as you're not measuring the wrong thing.

Key Takeaways

- Keeping a visual track of your habit is hugely satisfying because you get to watch your progress accumulate. This motivates you to continue.

- A habit tracker is a simple but effective way to keep track of your habit's progress.

- Clear's mantra for sticking to your habits is "never miss twice." It's okay to slip up once as long as you bounce back as quickly as possible.
- It is very important not to break the chain. Bad days are better than no-shows.
- When it comes to habit tracking, be careful not to measure the wrong parameters. Numbers are not the only way to monitor your progress.

Over to You

Think about which of your habits would benefit most from being tracked. Perhaps one you're finding particularly difficult? Or one that you are most proud of? Write out a few action statements using Clear's formula of habit tracking + habit-stacking:

"After [CURRENT HABIT], I will [TRACK MY HABIT]."

#1

After ______________________________, I will ______________________________.

#2

After ______________________________, I will ______________________________.

#3

After ______________________________, I will ______________________________.

Now create your own habit tracker (see the example below). It would be best to buy a separate calendar/notepad/diary for this purpose. That way, you will have more space to track your habit over a longer period of time. If you prefer the Paper Clip Strategy, set up a visual means to track your habit using two glass jars and 100 or so small, movable items.

	Jan	Feb	Mar	Apr	May	Jun	Jul	Aug	Sep	Oct	Nov	Dec
1												
2												
3												
4												
5												
6												
7												
8												
9												
10												
11												
12												
13												
14												
15												
16												
17												
18												
19												
20												
21												
22												
23												
24												
25												
26												
27												
28												
29												
30												
31												
Total												

Chapter 17: How an Accountability Partner Can Change Everything

Chapter Summary

In the previous chapters, Clear talks about making your good habits satisfying by providing immediate rewards. In this chapter, he looks at what happens when you invert this law: Make it unsatisfying. Now, it is all about making a bad habit painful. Bear in mind the Cardinal Rule from Chapter 15: if you want a habit to be avoided, you must immediately punish it.

Pain is just as powerful a motivator as pleasure. If we make failure painful, it is much more likely to get fixed. Restaurants are motivated to serve good food because they don't want bad reviews to threaten their business. A hairdresser has to do a good job otherwise they will never get returning customers. The graver the consequences, the quicker and more thoroughly we learn how to avoid them.

When the costs of a bad habit are felt immediately, it is even more effective. The reason we repeat bad habits is that they reward us with some sort of immediate satisfaction or pleasure *before* we feel the negative consequences. If we can close this gap between cause and effect, we have a shot at real change.

Clear notes that if you are going to rely on punishment to improve your behavior, it must be severe enough to actually deter you, and you need to make sure it is adequately enforced. He comes up with a simple but effective way to implement this: a Habit Contract (p. 167).

This is a contract you make with yourself where you state the habit you intend to do and the punishment you face if you fail to stick to it. You must then find one or two people to act as witnesses to this statement and enforce the punishment if necessary. Clear calls them accountability partners. The agreement can be made verbally or in writing, and all parties must sign it.

For example, if you wanted to build a walking habit, your Habit Contract might read as follows: "I will walk for 10 minutes every day for the next three months. Every time I miss a day, I will give $50 to my partner." Your partner, and anyone else you wanted to involve—a walking buddy or personal trainer perhaps—would then have to sign the contract with you, and they would act as your accountability partners.

Your contract could be much more detailed than that, with a step-by-step plan about where you were going to walk, at what time, and with whom, etc., but those are the basics. Once you've reached that goal, you could make another, more ambitious contract. You could train for a 10K walk, for example. Just remember, stepping up the goal means stepping up the immediate punishment.

A Habit Contract might seem like an unnecessary waste of time, but by treating the contract seriously, you treat your habit seriously. Even if you don't want to write it out and sign it, Clear says that at least having an accountability partner can be really useful. This can be as simple as having a running buddy or taking it in turns with someone to drive to the spot where your mutual habit takes place. Knowing that someone else is relying on you is a powerful enforcer because, now, it's not just you that you're letting down; it's your friends too.

Key Takeaways

- Pain is a powerful motivator. When the costs of a bad habit are felt immediately, we are much less likely to repeat it.
- A Habit Contract is a verbal or written contract you make with yourself and one or two others. You state the actions you intend to do and the punishment you face if you fail to stick to them. All parties sign.
- An accountability partner is an effective way to face the consequences of your actions immediately. We are motivated to act when people watch us because we care about our reputation and upholding our promises to other people.
- When you invert the Fourth Law of Behavior Change, you get: Make it unsatisfying (p. 169).

Over to You

Think about a habit that you are either finding really hard to stick to or really hard to shake. You may need to resort to more drastic measures to deal with it. Create a Habit Contract for yourself, making it as detailed as you want. Think about who you could recruit as an accountability partner. It is important to choose someone who is going to take their role seriously. It might be a good idea to ask a second person as well—someone whose opinion really matters to you.

Once you have written your contract out and everyone has signed it, put your words into action! You can use the space below for your first contract. Remember, for this to work, you have to really commit to the contract and be honest with yourself. When choosing a punishment, make sure that it's not too soft that you won't take it seriously and not too exaggerated that it could be distressing.

Sticking to your habit should feel more official now, especially as you have involved a third party who will hold you accountable.

<u>My Habit Contract</u>

My goal:

The habit(s) I will use to reach this goal:

In the event that I do not stick to this habit(s), my punishment is as follows:

Name and signature of contract owner:

Name and signature of accountability partner #1:

Name and signature of accountability partner #2 (if applicable):

Date:

Advanced Tactics: How to Go from Being Merely Good to Being Truly Great

Chapter 18: The Truth About Talent (When Genes Matter and When They Don't)

Chapter Summary

Having discussed the Four Laws of Behavior Change (make it obvious, make it attractive, make it easy, and make it satisfying), Clear now moves on to some more general advice about how to optimize your habits. Firstly, he mentions the importance of being tactical. Choose a habit that naturally aligns with your skills and abilities. This is going to make it easier and more satisfying to carry out.

Clear says we must accept the fact that we are born with different abilities. The trick is not to bemoan this fact but to utilize it. Our genetic makeup does not determine whether we will be successful or not; it simply gives us an advantage in some situations and a disadvantage in others. For example, being five feet tall is incredibly useful if you want to be a jockey or a gymnast, but it's not going to do you any favors if you want to be a basketball player.

If you want to be successful, place yourself in an environment where your natural talents will shine. Once you discover you're good at something, the joy and delight that follow are a powerful motivator to continue. So how do you find out which habits are naturally suited to you? Clear says first you must understand your personality.

Research has shown that genes influence every aspect of our behavior, predisposing us to certain personality types. These personalities will in turn influence the habits we pick up. For instance, someone born with higher levels of oxytocin will tend to have a warmer, more compassionate personality. You can imagine this person developing habits like organizing dinner parties or sending postcards to friends and family. Likewise, someone who indicates low levels of extroversion might be more naturally inclined to build solo habits like reading or gaming.

Of course, our personality is not the only component that influences our habits, but it certainly plays a big part. Clear notes that you don't have to feel guilty or ashamed about your personality, but you do need to understand it and—most importantly—work with it. If you want to learn an instrument but all the obvious options haven't worked for you—like piano and guitar—go for something different like percussion or choir singing. If you want to start a reading habit but you find it difficult to concentrate, try comics and graphic novels first, or perhaps audiobooks if that doesn't work. No one option is better or more impressive than the other; it's whatever version works best for you.

Once you've considered your personality, the next thing to think about is what comes easily to you. This is important because if you find something easy, you will most likely be highly competent at it. The praise you receive for doing a good job will make you happy and motivate you to work harder, eventually leading to promotions and pay raises. And so it continues. But how do you know what's easy and what's difficult?

Clear says one way to figure this out is by using a strategy he calls the "explore/exploit trade-off" (p. 178). This is essentially a more efficient version of trial and error. It starts with an exploration stage, where you do some light research on a wide variety of different fields. After you've done this for a little while, narrow your attention down to the areas that interest you the most and seem to come easier to you. If it goes well, start exploiting this area. If you're still struggling, continue to explore other possibilities.

Clear says the ratio of exploit to explore should eventually get to roughly 8:2 or 9:1. In other words, spend 80-90 percent of your time working in an area that delivers the best results and 10-20 percent exploring other projects. As per the 80/20 rule, this might vary slightly depending on your age and what stage you're at in your career.

Finally, if you can't find an environment that favors your natural abilities, design your own. Many successful people have gotten to where they are because they created their own niche. This significantly reduces your competition and allows you to specialize in your field.

All this being said, Clear reminds his readers that any route they take will require hard work. Playing to our genetic predispositions does not mean doing less work, it merely clarifies what direction we need to go in. It helps us to realize where our time and energy will be best spent. Forget about comparing yourself to others, focus on fulfilling your own potential instead.

Key Takeaways

- The key to success is to choose habits that naturally align with your skills and abilities.
- Our genes do not determine our success; they simply give us an advantage in some situations and a disadvantage in others. Choose an environment that plays to your strengths.
- Aligning your new behavior with your personality will help you to build a habit that sticks.
- Use Clear's strategy of exploring and exploiting to discover what comes easiest to you. If you are currently flowing and winning, you have to exploit. If you are still struggling, you have to continue to explore.
- If you can't find an environment that favors your natural abilities, design your own.
- Playing to our genetic predispositions does not mean doing less work, it merely clarifies where our time and energy will be best spent.

Over to You

The following questions are taken from Clear's book (pp. 178-179). They are designed to help you narrow down areas of natural skill and ability. Write your ideas down below, leaving your answers underneath each question.

This is a very useful exercise for discerning which habits are best suited to you. As a general rule, writing things down can really help to clarify and organize your thoughts. Simple actions like writing a list of skills and interests can provide the insights you need to start making life and career choices.

Q1: What feels like fun to me, but work to others?

Q2: What makes me lose track of time?

Q3: Where do I get greater returns than the average person?

Q4: What comes naturally to me?

The work does not end with these questions. You should continue to practice introspection and think honestly about your habits—which ones are going well and which ones are a struggle. This is a necessary step towards discovering your true essence. If you ever feel frustrated, remember to be compassionate with yourself.

Perhaps you have simply chosen a habit that is not best suited to you.

To give an example from this author's own life, I always used to watch motivational videos that stated that waking up at 6 a.m., 4 a.m., and even 3 a.m. would boost your productivity and change your life. I tried to embrace those habits—and was successful for a while—but the good streak would never last.

Then one day, I read about circadian rhythms in *Why We Sleep* by Matthew Walker and discovered that some people's body clocks are set differently. I realized that being a night owl was simply in my nature and that night owls are unfairly judged by society. So I stopped being ashamed about working at night.

With this newfound acceptance of myself, I changed my schedule to alternate between two cycles: noon–1 a.m. or 8 p.m.–9 a.m. I still wake up early, but I don't put pressure on myself if it's not that early. Having heard this, you might like to do your own research regarding some of your habits.

Additionally, I would recommend you look into different personality types to gain some insights about your own. Start by taking a few different personality tests and see what comes up. The Big Five or 16Personalities test are great places to start.

Chapter 19: The Goldilocks Rule: How to Stay Motivated in Life and Work

Chapter Summary

The question of why some people can stick to their habits and others can't is one that still evades scientists and researchers. Although not fully answered, a finding that has come up again and again is this: for a task to stay motivating, it must be of "just manageable difficulty" (p. 183). In other words, your brain likes it neither too easy nor too hard. Hence the name "the Goldilocks Rule."

This means you have to make sure a habit is easy enough to pick up at the beginning and then—once the behavior is well established—challenging enough to sustain your interest and engagement. You can achieve this by increasing the level of difficulty slowly—just enough that you feel you are continually making progress. The optimal result is that you hit a "flow state" (p. 185). This is the feeling of being fully immersed in something.

All of this is to keep the enemy at bay: boredom. Clear remarks that boredom is "perhaps the greatest villain on the quest for self-improvement" (p. 185). More than failure or humiliation, learning how to overcome the obstacle of boredom is what separates the truly successful from the rest. Because, unfortunately, boredom is part and parcel of the habit-building process.

As we have seen, a habit needs to be repeated many times before it can be mastered. This means that a degree of monotony is inevitable. Once the initial excitement wears off, our enthusiasm flags, and our brains look to other areas for novelty. This leads us to miss a day or skip a routine, which doesn't feel like a big deal because we've practiced our habit every day that week. We tell ourselves, "Things are going well; I think it's safe to take a break."

This need for continual novelty is exploited by industries like fast food, porn, and video gaming, all of which create highly habit-forming products. The psychological term for it is "variable rewards" (p. 186). This is when you receive a reward some of the time but not always, and never in a way that you can predict. Arcade machines are the best example of this. They are so successful because they have found a way to circumvent boredom. Let the customer win just enough times to be satisfied, and lose just enough times to sustain the desire to win.

The Goldilocks Rule works in the same way with your habits. Give yourself enough of a challenge to keep things interesting, but make sure you're also making gains and feeling rewarded. No matter how hard we try, however, Clear says we all have to come up against boredom at some point on our journey. When this happens, it's about working through the boredom and putting in the reps anyway. A true professional will stick to their habits no matter what their mood is. They are devoted to the importance of the practice. The trick, Clear says, is to learn to love boredom.

Key Takeaways

- The Goldilocks Rule states that to sustain motivation we must work on tasks that are not too easy and not too hard; ideally just below the limit of our current abilities.
- To stick to a habit, give yourself enough of a challenge to keep things interesting, but make sure you're also making gains and feeling rewarded.
- Boredom is the true enemy of progress. Unfortunately, boredom is inevitable once a habit becomes routine.

- Learning how to work through the boredom and put the reps in—no matter what their mood—is what separates professionals from amateurs.

Over to You

Think about how you could apply the Goldilocks Rule to your habits. Perhaps pick a few habits that you can see becoming boring more quickly than others. Brainstorm some ideas of how you could build on those habits to keep them exciting. It doesn't have to be a comprehensive, step-by-step plan at this point—just initial ideas.

This way, whenever you come up against boredom in your real-life practice, you have a repository of ideas on hand to keep things interesting. A first example has been given to help you.

Habit	**Ideas for Progression**
Rollerblading	Start by rollerblading down my street. Once I've practiced this for a week, I can expand to rollerblading around my block. Once I'm confident with rollerblading around my local area, I will cycle to different areas of the city (quiet neighborhoods only) and practice there. This should sustain me for at least a month. When I'm at home, I can work on playlists to listen to while I rollerblade (one earplug in only for safety). Search for funky, upbeat songs. Once I've nailed going forward, I can start practicing rollerblading backward—maybe even doing turns and jumps. To practice, I will go back to my own street to start with.

	Other ideas: Consider going to skateparks, plazas, or large open spaces to practice rollerblading over obstacles. Join a rollerblading group, enter a competition, and experience rollerblading in other cities/countries.

Chapter 20: The Downside of Creating Good Habits

Chapter Summary

In this final chapter, Clear looks at the risks we face when building habits. Once a habit becomes automatic, we cease to think about it consciously. As we have seen in Chapters 3 and 11, this is a useful and smart strategy. However, it can also be a pitfall. If we simply repeat things mindlessly, we could be making the same mistakes over and over again without realizing it. Just because you repeat a habit doesn't mean you're improving it. Once you stop paying attention, you stall your progress.

Of course, this is not a concern for all habits. Many can be done somewhat mindlessly, and it won't cause any harm. As Clear says, you don't need to keep improving how you brush your teeth or tie your shoelaces. For the habits that you want to excel in, however, a more focused approach is required. Clear comes up with a formula for this:

"Habits + Deliberate Practice = Mastery" (p. 190).

Essentially, this involves a two-fold process:

1. Build up a habit through repetition until you can do all of the basics automatically.
2. Once you have this foundational level mastered, you can turn your efforts to specializing in a particular area.

Once you have repeated this specialized behavior enough times, it too becomes automatic, and you are ready for the next level. In this way, you advance by building your habits on top of each other in a continual cycle until you reach the highest levels of mastery.

When you feel like you're really getting a grip on mastering your habits, that's the moment to check your awareness and make sure you're not becoming complacent. Clear has a strategy for this, which he calls "reflection and review" (p. 192). This is a system for reviewing your performance at regular intervals. How often you do it is up to you—it could be once a month, it could be twice a year. The important part is that you are reflecting on your progress and checking for mistakes and possible areas for improvement.

At the end of each year, Clear asks himself three questions (p. 195):

1. What went well this year?
2. What didn't go so well this year?
3. What did I learn?

This allows him to reflect on his progress, namely what he achieved and/or didn't achieve. Six months later, he checks in again and asks himself (p. 195):

1. What are the core values that drive my life and work?
2. How am I living and working with integrity right now?
3. How can I set a higher standard in the future?

This allows him to check in with the type of person he aspires to be and see if his behavior is reflecting that identity. By conducting this biannual review, Clear is monitoring two very important things: (1) that his habits are on track and remain productive, and (2) that they align with his desired identity.

While emphasizing not to lose sight of their identity, Clear also warns his readers not to become consumed by it either. When we invest too deeply in an idea of who we are, we hold ourselves back from true growth. To avoid this, keep your identity loose and adaptable. Don't let one single aspect define you, but rather maintain a set of core values that can apply to any role you might take on. For example, "I'm the director" becomes "I'm the type of person who is organized, efficient, and can lead a team." Maintaining a degree of flexibility is crucial in a world that is ever-changing.

Key Takeaways

- Once a habit becomes automatic, we cease to think about it consciously. The downside to this is we risk repeating the same mistakes and stalling our progress.
- Clear's formula for excelling in a habit is: "Habits + Deliberate Practice = Mastery." Mastery unlocks the next stage of performance.
- "Reflection and review" is Clear's system for maintaining a regular awareness of your performance. It allows you to keep your habits on track and ensure they align with your desired identity.
- Investing in one single version of yourself will hold you back from true growth. Keep your identity adaptable while maintaining a set of core values.

Over to You

Now that you've reached the end of this workbook, you will have made a number of action plans to get your habits up and running. One final exercise is therefore in order. Once you've made a start on implementing your new habits, set up a date and time for yourself to sit, reflect, and review your progress. How soon you do this is up to you, but I would suggest two to three months after starting your habit. This way, you leave enough time to make progress without waiting so long that you lose the motivation to follow through.

After this first session, you can increase the amount of time in between reviews and focus on fully embracing the habit itself. Repeat them as often as you see fit. As you saw above, Clear does it only twice a year, and that is sufficient. You can use the questions Clear asks himself as a starting point if you like, but make sure you are asking questions that are relevant and meaningful to you.

Write down the date and time of your first review below to make it official. Also, write down the questions that you will regularly ask yourself, keeping in mind these two key factors: Are my habits on track? Am I reinforcing my desired identity? Take your time with this.

My First Review

Date:

Time:

Questions I will ask myself:

Now that you have an official date with the questions written down, write a letter to yourself with your current answers to these questions included. This letter is to be opened on the date you selected, but only AFTER you've completed the review.

Also include in your letter how you are feeling in this current moment and where you think you're heading in your life. Capture anything else you want. This will make things more interesting when you open the letter and compare your different states. It might make the review more insightful.

Leave this letter in a safe place but where you can still see it (visual cue). Resist the temptation to open it before the review date. If done well, the results could be surprising. It might move you to take up this letter-writing habit in the long run. The more time you leave in between letters, the more interesting the insights will be.

Conclusion: The Secrets to Results That Last

Armed with the Four Laws of Behavior Change—and all the tools and strategies that come with them—you are more than equipped to go away and implement successful, long-lasting habits. If you commit to the practice of continually making one percent improvements, you will be rewarded in a big way.

Clear leaves his readers with a couple of reminders here. Firstly, focus on your systems and not the end goal. And secondly, self-improvement is a continuous process. Never stop improving; progress is a circle, not a straight line. This is the secret to results that last.

One small change won't transform your life. When stacked on top of a thousand other small changes, however, it will. This is the nature of atomic habits. They compound into life-changing results.

You have already taken the first and biggest step on your habit-building journey, now it's time to decide if you will take the second step, **implementation**.

Dear Reader

I want to personally thank you for choosing this book from among dozens out there, for acquiring an authorized copy of it and supporting my work, and for making it all the way to the end.

If you liked the content, please consider posting a review or rating on Amazon, it would mean a lot to me and it would help others benefit from my work. It is also the best way to support our team and independent writers like myself.

Thank you.

References

Clear, J. (n.d.). *30 Days to Better Habits Workbook.* jamesclear.s3.amazonaws.com/Habits+Course/30+Days+to+Better+Habits+Workbook.pdf

Clear, J. (2019). *ATOMIC HABITS: an Easy and Proven Way to Build Good Habits and Break Bad Ones*. Penguin Random House.

Nicole. (2021, September 6). *Atomic Habits Cheat Sheet Printables, Worksheets & Summary*. 101 Planners. 101planners.com/atomic-habits/

Silvestre, D. (n.d.). *Atomic Habits by James Clear: Summary and Lessons*. Dan Silvestre. Retrieved March 16, 2023, from dansilvestre.com/summaries/atomic-habits-james-clear/

Made in the USA
Coppell, TX
12 March 2024

30057875R10085